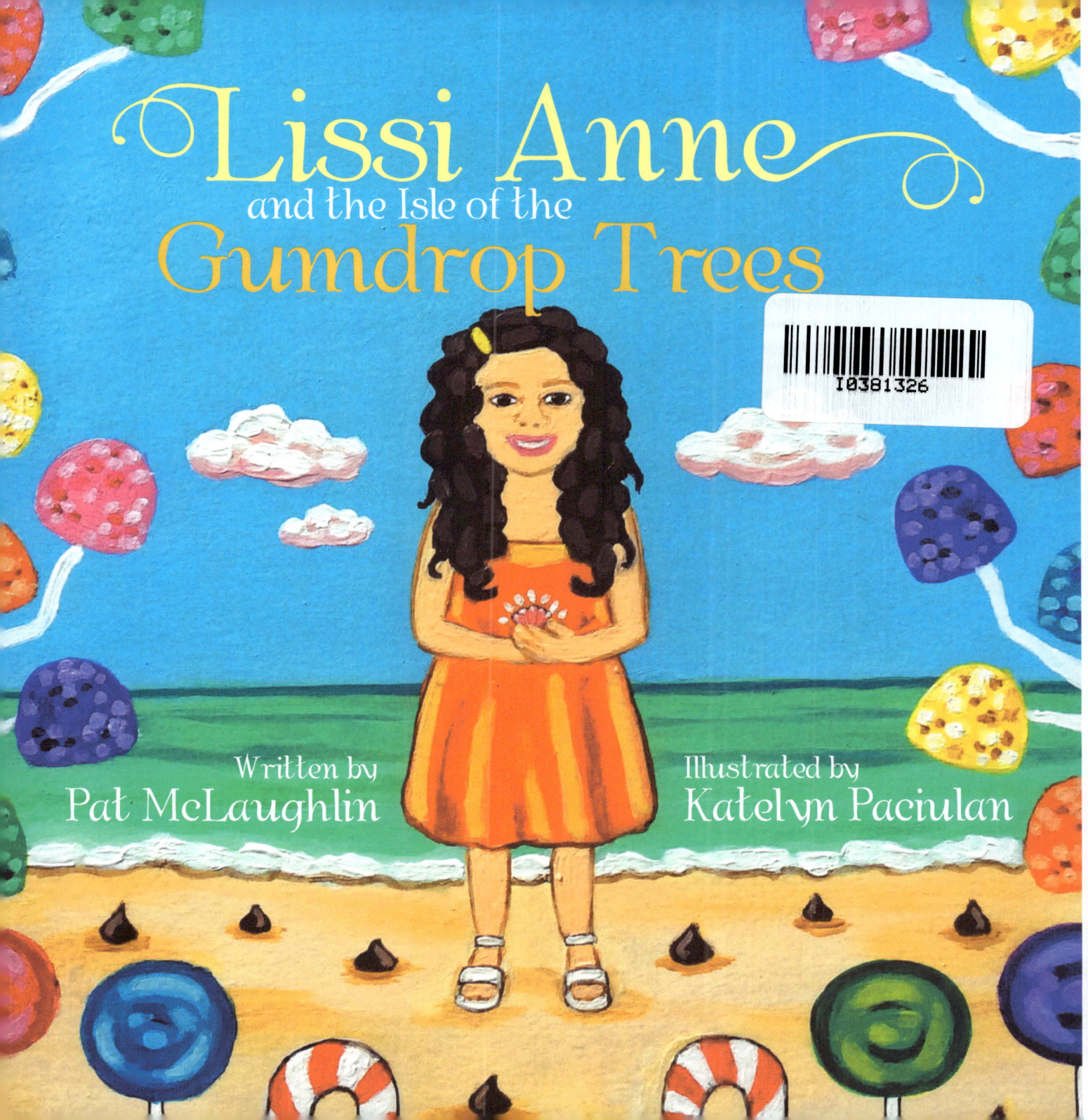

Copyright © 2020 by Pat McLaughlin.

ISBN-978-1-6485-8523-4

All rights reserved. No part of this book may be reproduced or transmitted in any form or by any means, electronic or mechanical, including photocopying, recording, or by any information storage and retrieval system, without permission in writing from the copyright owner.

The views expressed in this work are solely those of the author and do not necessarily reflect the views of the publisher, and the publisher hereby disclaims any responsibility for them.

Matchstick Literary
1-888-306-8885
orders@matchliterary.com

Acknowledgement

Jim, my children, and my loving grandchildren, many countless thanks for your continued love and support. Norbert, Carolyn, Nate, Sherri, Charlotte, Nick, Jenny, Nelson and Nicole, many years ago we bonded into one big family and will always be there for one another for years to come. Patti and Rex, your example of love for family is so genuinely heartwarming. Angi, Travis, Kylie, Bryson, Julie, Jamieson, Easton and Krystal, I hold you all so dear to my heart. My dear soul-mate Lisa and Dylan, what would our lives have been like if we hadn't found the way into each other's souls? Madeline, you extended a hand in friendship so many years ago, and this bond still goes on today. Thanks to you, Wayne, Clare, Sean, Corinne and Ciara for the "Céad Míle Fáilte" that flows from your hearts every day. Finally, many thanks to Kate for her beautiful illustrations that help my words come to life.

Dedication

This book is dedicated to one of my beautiful grandchildren, Alyssa Breighann. You take a world filled with so many twists and turns and set it straight with one of your smiles. We can all learn a lesson of love and compassion from you. Lissi, may you always believe in magical lands and have many good friends to share your life with because life is only good if we make it so.

Down by the seashore where the waves meet the sand
playing there among the rocks is Little Lissi Anne.

The tiny crabs crawl all about and wiggle 'tween her toes.
She jumps and shouts a gleeful cheer everywhere she goes.

One sunny day while playing, a friend came crawling by.
She stopped along her busy way to say a happy "Hi."

Now Giselle, as she was called by name, lived deep within the sea,
but sometimes she would take a stroll to visit with Lissi.

Seeing Lissi Anne that day, Giselle crawled up to talk,
and as we know she has no feet so she did the "lobster-walk".

"Good morning Lissi Anne," she said as a smile lit up her face.
"It's good to visit on this fine morn and in this special place.

I brought you something; it's just for you, I dug it up with care.
It's in my claw to keep it safe; I had to put it there."

She opened up her big brown claw; the treasure was within.
It was a special seashell, very frail and very thin.

"This is a good luck charm for you, so cherish it with care.
With this you can go 'round the world, you can travel anywhere."

Lissi Anne jumped up with joy; she knew where she would go,
for she had dreamt about this trip for a million years or so.

A boat made from a fallen star sat there upon the sand.
Always ready to raise her sail, this boat, "The Lissi Anne."

She climbed on board, waved goodbye; she was finally on her way.
"The Lissi Anne" floated out to sea; to and fro it gently swayed.

She clapped her hands and danced a jig upon the open seas.
She was on her way to the land of fun, the Isle of the Gumdrop Trees.

She steered that boat straight and long as swiftly it did flow,
until through glasses she did spy the Gumdrop Trees aglow.

The boat was guided to the shore pushed gently by the wind.
She jumped on out and looked about not sure where to begin.

The roads were lined with Gumdrop Trees with stars that twinkled bright,
and from their branches hung rows of candy much to her delight.

The streets were made of taffy stretched awfully thin and fine,
and streetlights of colored lollipops were standing in a line.

Fences made from candy canes in twists of red and white,
surrounded houses glowing warm from minty-butter lights.

Benches made from chocolate drops, which one could sit upon,
to watch the rows of candy roses sprout across the lawn.

A flowing, bubbling, chocolate lake was part of this sweet town;
Frogs sat upon cream-butter pads with smiles and never frowns.

A fountain made from soda pop, a cool and dandy treat,
helps to swallow all the sweets that one had chanced to eat.

Fluffy clouds of marshmallows floated gently through the air,
while flavored-colored rainbows from time to time appeared.

Lissi Anne just stood and stared at all these awesome sights.
It made her head swim round and round and filled her with delight.

Now, Lissi Anne was not the only child who came to town;
there were many happy children scattered all around.

She romped around all that day while eating such a feast.
It was her greatest holiday to say the very least.

She made so many special friends and had such wondrous fun
that she didn't even notice the dreadful setting of the sun.

The isle was finally going down to a really needed sleep.
Lissi Anne was so very sad that she began to weep.

Then suddenly she remembered the grand day that she just had,
A smile lit up across her face..... she was no longer sad.

She climbed aboard that little boat and started her trip back.
She placed some of the goodies into a paper sack.

There were gumdrops, flavored lollipops, and chocolate drops galore
to share with all her friends and family back upon the shore.

And when at last she finally docked that golden treasured ship,
she knew that she would never forget this very tasty trip.

When she reached into her pocket, her treasure was still there
that frail and tiny seashell; she handled with great care.

This everlasting journey she'll remember oh so well.
She'll remember too that it was a gift from her loving friend, Giselle.

She'll forever treasure this fine gift and use it now and then
when she decides she needs to visit her special place again.